what your pet

is trying

to tell you

DOG
SPEAK

 sourcebooks

Sourcebooks and the colophon are registered
trademarks of Sourcebooks.

Published by Sourcebooks
P.O. Box 4410, Naperville, Illinois 60567-4410
(630) 961-3900
sourcebooks.com

Originally published in 2022 in the United Kingdom by LOM
ART, an imprint of Michael O'Mara Books Limited.

Cataloging-in-Publication Data is on file with the Library of Congress.

Printed and bound in China.
WKT 10 9 8 7 6 5 4 3 2 1

DOG SPEAK

What your pet is trying to tell you

Written by Liz Marvin
Illustrated by Yelena Bryksenkova

sourcebooks

INTRODUCTION

Lifting a paw, taking a bow, sleeping on their back, stealing your socks…our best furry friends may not be able to tell us what they are thinking and feeling, but they certainly have lots of ways to show us!

Dogs and people have an amazing history together—archaeologists think we may go back thirty thousand years! Over this time, we have become the perfect companions and the best of friends. But even so, misunderstandings between our species do happen. Our dogs find it hard to fathom how we manage without tails, and they are often surprised when their carefully selected gift of a frog from the garden does not get the warm reception they expected.

Each dog has their own personality and will communicate in a way that is unique to them. Just like people, some dogs are naturally ebullient and expressive, and it's easy to know what they're feeling, whereas others can be a bit more reserved. And different breeds have varying approaches

4

to communication too—after all, what a collie can say with their ears isn't going to work for a spaniel.

But at the same time, if you are lucky enough to have made a few canine chums, you'll have noticed there's a doggy language that is pretty common to most of them. And if we really pay attention, then we can start to figure out what our dogs are trying to tell us, whether your fuzzy buddy is anxious, bored, excited, or they've just really had it with the cat.

These pages are a celebration of doggy behavior and the amazing, life-affirming, and sometimes hilarious relationships we have with our beloved hounds. We may never be able to tell what exactly is going on behind those big brown eyes, but if we look carefully, we might be able to pick up some clues. What is your dog saying to you?

THE HAIR-RAISER

When we say a human has their hackles up, we usually mean they're annoyed about something and about to go on the offensive. But that's not always the case for our pooches. Hair raised on a dog's back can indicate they are upset or stressed, but it might also mean they are excited or even just a bit confused. It's an involuntary reaction—like goose bumps for us—so you'll need to have a look at your furry friend's body language to try to figure out what's up.

THE BED INVASION

You've just bought your puppy the coziest dog bed that money can buy, so *why* do they bound straight upstairs and get onto your bed? The simple answer is that they just want to be close

to you. Your bed smells like you—and also like them if they get to sleep there often. Your dog thinks that you are both part of the same pack, and packs that snooze together, stay together.

THE BACK SLEEPER

This chill puppy has their legs in the air because they just don't care. This sleeping posture is your dog saying it's the weekend, and they are well and truly off duty. When your hardworking hound is zonked out on their back with their stomach exposed, it means they are totally relaxed and feel safe; they know they've got nothing to worry about. Tummy rub, please?

11

THE FLOPPY TONGUE

Doggy tongues are pretty amazing things —in fact, dogs often look at humans and wonder how we can possibly manage with our tiny tongues. A hot pooch will stick out their tongue and pant to help cool down, but the tongue can tell you other things about how your dog is feeling. When they are relaxed, their mouth muscles will be too, meaning their tongue will often loll adorably out of the side of their big grinning face.

THE SIDE SLEEPER

When your dog catches some z's lying sprawled out on their side, you know that they are happy and calm. They are not expecting to have to spring up quickly and investigate strange noises or protect you from harm—all is well in this puppy's world. It also leaves their paws free to twitch and pedal as they dream doggy dreams of muddy puddles and chasing balls.

THE SNEEZE

Ges-hound-heit! Dogs' noses are up to one hundred thousand times more sensitive than ours, scientists say, so it's no surprise that sometimes something just gets up there and tickles. But sneezing may be a signal that your doggy is concentrating, a sign they are frustrated, or simply their way of reassuring you that they are only playing in a rough game. Have a look around to see if you can figure out what they are trying to tell you.

THE FOX

Just like people, individual dogs often have a preference for the position in which they like to fall asleep. But when your pet curls up with their paws tucked up and their tail wrapped around, it might simply be because they are cold, or maybe they feel a bit scared or unsafe. This is how their doggy ancestors would have slept, and so curling up in a ball is an instinctive habit left over from our pets' wild days.

THE GIFT

While your pooch might not always act like they think you're in charge, dropping a favorite toy—or one of your shoes they've helpfully chewed—at your feet is a sign that they see you as the alpha of the family and want to make you happy. It's also a way to get your attention or show that they want to play. Unfortunately, dogs are not the savviest gift givers—it might be something they found in the neighbor's trash that they use to get the message across.

THE LEAN

A gentle lean against your legs is all about attention. It can be a subtle rebuke from your dog when they feel like they're not getting enough from you or they're feeling insecure. Or for some breeds, like whippets and greyhounds, it's actually their way of giving *you* some attention —in dog speak, they are saying, "I would give you a hug right now if I had arms."

THE HEAD TILT

This pose makes even the naughtiest doggy look thoughtful and attentive to our human gaze. Experts think that when dogs tilt their heads, it's to hear better or to figure out where a sound might be coming from. So that inquisitive look could be saying, "Huh? What's that now? Did someone say *biscuit*?"

THE TAIL CHASE

Puppies chase their tails in play and to find out more about this funny waggy thing following them around. An older dog might just be having a bit of fun, especially if they know it makes you laugh. However, it can also be a sign that your fuzzy friend is bored and needs some stimulation. Go on, you've got time for a quick game of fetch!

THE FULL-BODY WAG

This one's not rocket science! When a dog is
very happy to see you and wants to play, then
sometimes the tail is not enough, and it seems
like all of them is wagging away in a big old full-
body wiggle that even a human can't mistake.
Is there anything nicer than a joyful puppy
giving it their all when you walk in the door?

THE POST BATH CRAZIES

Different dogs have different views on bathtime. Often a pooch that jumped gleefully into a pond just hours before is nowhere to be found once the showerhead starts cranking. Most dogs find the

experience at least a bit stressful and will zoom around the house afterwards in relief that it's all over – and to get dry too, no matter how many times you try to explain the concept of a "towel." Plus there's always the hope that you might chase them, which would be so much more fun than standing in the tub covered in doggy shampoo.

THE SQUINT

Does your four-legged friend ever pull a face at you like they're trying to read the last line on an eye test? In happy dogs, squinting is a sign of what trainers call *appeasement* —or body language that they hope might calm a potentially tricky situation. So if your squinty dog has recently been at the cat's food again, it could be that they feel bad and are hoping you'll forgive them.

THE DIG

For some dogs, there is no lawn that can't be improved by a muddy hole. Terriers in particular often enjoy a good dig. Sometimes, though, this can be a sign that your dog is bored and feeling a bit *Shawshank Redemption* out there in the back garden. First check you don't have a mole infestation they are simply trying to bring to your attention; if not, then maybe a few extra walks are in order.

THE ONE-PAW LIFT

Dogs have always found their human's insistence that they learn to "shake hands" confusing, as for them, saying hello means investigating a completely different part of their new acquaintance's anatomy. When your furry friend lifts one paw, it usually means that they are uncertain or anticipating something. So rather than, "Delighted to see you again," they are actually asking, "When's dinner?"

THE LICK

It's the ultimate doggy way of showing affection, and we humans tend to like our pets' enthusiastic sloppy kisses. When our happy pooch goes in for a big lick to the face with their ears forward and tail wagging, they're showing you lots of love, and they know they will get a reaction from you. Though it's not *all* about the love. We smell and taste fascinating to dogs, so when they greet you with a big lick, they might also be trying to figure out where you've been all day and what you had for lunch.

THE SMILE

Is there anything better than a happy doggy with a massive grin on its face? When a dog has an upturned mouth, tongue hanging out, lips pulled back, it looks so much like a human

smile that we just can't resist. There's not much research to tell us what's really going on here; scientists think that it could be a result of our long-shared history with our canine buddies, and that they make that face because on some level they know we like it. But most dog owners would disagree—they know when their dog is giving them a big contented grin.

41

THE JUMP UP

Your dog thinks you should be thrilled that they excitedly cover you in kisses and almost knock you over the second you get home; you would prefer to get in the door without being assailed by muddy paws and a big doggy tongue. Jumping up can be a way of trying to assert dominance, but it can also just be your dog saying, "Look at meeeee!" Obviously, how much of a problem this is depends on what kind of dog you have – an excitable chihuahua is a different proposition than an overenthusiastic Saint Bernard.

THE STIFF UPWARDS TAIL

▽△▽△▽△▽△▽△▽△ ▽△▽△▽△▽△

Even if a dog seems to be wagging their tail slightly, that doesn't necessarily mean all is well in their world. A tall, stiffly held tail often means a dog is uncomfortable, anxious, or maybe even aggressive. If you see a dog in the park that is standing very still with their tail in this position and maybe moving it slightly, it's usually wise to give them lots of space, just in case something has spooked them or they're having a bad day.

THE HARD STARE

An unblinking dog may be a little intimidating, but in fact it is more likely that when your dog is staring at you, they are actually just trying to get your attention or make a connection. When a dog and their human stare into each other's eyes,

there's a hormonal response from our four-legged friends, and eye contact can deepen their emotional bond with us. Of course, if you're holding a treat and your dog is staring at you, it's all about the biscuit.

THE EYE AVOIDANCE

Is there anything more heartwarming than your pup gazing up at you lovingly with their big trusting eyes? (Even if you know that they are actually thinking, "Can I share your dinner?") However, though your hound might be happy to lock eyes with their favorite human most of the time, in the doggy world, prolonged direct eye contact is usually a challenge and a way to assert dominance. So your dog might be avoiding your gaze because they think it's polite, or it might be because they feel uncomfortable. Perhaps they know you will be treading in something unpleasant when you go into your bedroom later…

THE YAWN

When a dog yawns, you might assume they were plagued by cat-filled nightmares and didn't get much sleep the night before. But not so—in fact, dogs yawn for a number of reasons that have nothing to do with feeling sleepy. Sometimes it can be a sign of stress, sometimes a signal to other overexcited dogs around them to calm down, but also hint that they're anticipating something fun. So, next time your dog yawns, don't crush their hopes with an early bedtime.

THE "I MISS YOU"

Have you ever walked in the door to find the sofa has been pulled apart, the remote chewed up, and all your shoes scattered across the floor? And in the middle of it all, one very

sheepish puppy? Your dog most likely knew they were not going to be very popular as a result, but they just couldn't help themselves. This can be a sign of separation anxiety, and while your fuzzy buddy would always rather you stayed home with them, most dogs get over it eventually with a bit of reassurance and training.

THE FREEZE

Dogs have their own version of the fight, flight, or freeze response that humans are familiar with. It can be easy to miss this subtle sign that your pet is feeling uneasy, as it might only last a couple of seconds, but a dog who stands stock-still is usually trying to assess a situation that's making them feel uncomfortable. Make sure they have the space and opportunity to walk away for a time-out if you can.

THE SHAKE-IT-OFF

The sudden full-body convulsion is your dog's
way of getting rid of excess adrenaline and/or
muscle tension when things have gotten a little

too exciting. You might notice them doing it after playtime with another dog or while rushing around the house waiting for their walk, when you finally clip the leash on. It's like a quick doggy system reboot—now they're good to go.

THE DROOLS

Some dogs are simply slobbery and proud—if your canine companion is a Newfoundland or basset hound, for example, you'll be used to every fetched ball being covered in drool. And if you're cooking a delicious-smelling steak, then naturally your puppy's mouth is going to water. But excess saliva in dogs can be a sign of stress. If they are also panting heavily or even trembling, but they haven't been running around, then it's likely something nearby is bothering them.

THE FIRM JAW

While a loose, floppy tongue and a relaxed mouth shows that your dog is feeling chill and happy, a mouth that's firmly closed indicates that they are on their guard. It can simply be a sign that they are sizing up a situation, so look at the rest of their body language to help you guess their mood. Are their ears back or hackles up? What do their eyes look like? Of course, they might just be lost in thoughts of squirrels.

THE SPIN
▽△▽△▽△▽△▽△▽△

Just like with the tail chase, some dogs will spin
around in a circle because they are clowning
around, trying to get your attention. Or it might
be that there is a lot going on in their minds; they
are dealing with too many doggy feelings and
their brains are—quite literally—going in circles.

THE NOSE LICK

Let's be honest, if you had a tongue that big, you'd probably be tempted to lick your nose, right? The nose lick has a practical function too—a dog's nose is very sensitive and gives them lots of info about what's going on around them. So, keeping it moist and in tip-top condition is an important job. A quick nose lick is also the canine way of taking a beat to assess the situation and decide what to do.

THE BELLY-UP

○○○○○○○○○○○○○○○○○○ ○○

Dogs mostly flop over on their backs for
one of two reasons. The first is submissive
behavior; they are showing that they know you

are in charge and making sure you understand they are not a threat. The second is because they just really, really want you to scratch their tummy—the one bit they can't reach to scratch themselves! It's easy to tell the difference if you pay attention—a dog wanting a belly rub is wiggly and relaxed, with a waggy tail and floppy tongue.

THE PLAY BOW

If you've ever been around a fun-loving doggo, you'll recognize this body language. A play bow is when your fuzzy friend puts their front legs out with elbows on the ground and bows down with

their butt in the air. They'll do it to other dogs in the park and to their humans too, to say, "I want to play!" Look out for this when two dogs are playing—even if the game gets a little rough, a play bow is a sign that it's still all in good fun.

THE READY-
FOR-ANYTHING

+ ✕ + ✕ + ✕ + ✕ + + ✕ + ✕

Looking at the tail, ears, and mouth all together is
the best way to get an insight into what your pet
is thinking and feeling. When their ears are high
and facing forward, their mouth is relaxed, and
their tail is ready to wag at a moment's notice,
then your doggy chum is feeling secure and ready
for the challenges of the day, be they squirrels,
cats, or postmen. (Not the vet though, obviously.)

THE FORWARD LEAN

Young dogs in particular go in for a forward lean—it's usually because they are interested and curious about something in their immediate environment. So long as they aren't showing any other body language that indicates they might be feeling stressed, then a straight pointed tail and forward ears as they poke their nose towards whatever has grabbed their attention show they are trying to figure something out.

THE SNARL

When a dog is baring their teeth, with their ears back, and even snarling, they are on high alert—your pet is feeling threatened and maybe angry. Fear and possession-aggression are often the main causes, so perhaps your dog is afraid of fireworks, or maybe they have just finally lost it with the cat eating out of their food bowl. Either way, this guy needs some space and for their boundaries to be respected.

THE RISING BARK

This is the sign of a doggy having a good time! It usually begins as a midpitch bark and is followed by some more that go up in pitch. Whether your dog is playing with their friends in the park or is just delighted to have found a particularly high-caliber stick, this is one excited and happy pooch who cannot keep their joy inside.

THE HOWL

While their wolf ancestors would howl to communicate with their pack or to announce their territory to any rivals in the vicinity, our domestic doggies are much more likely to be responding to a sound they can hear. Sometimes they might be singing along to the radio (or, let's face it, a car alarm), and sometimes they are complaining that it's annoying and hurting their ears. Less Bieber, more Snoop Dogg, please.

THE LOW GROWL

Growling doesn't always mean a dog is upset or angry—puppies often growl in play when they are learning to find their voices, and a happy mutt might make a low groany growl when they are enjoying themselves and feeling content. Knowing the difference between "This is nice" and "I'm deeply unimpressed" is all about listening carefully and watching the rest of the pup's body language.

THE HOT DOG

When you're covered in fur, staying warm is easy, but cooling down can be a bit more of an issue. It's not really in a dog's nature to lie flat on their back as it puts them in a vulnerable position (unless, of course, they are having a super-chill snooze—see The Back Sleeper). But the bit of a dog with the least fur is their tummy, so exposing it to the air is one way to cool down. They flop belly down in a muddy puddle in the park after an enthusiastic game of chase for the same reason—it's not always a sarcastic comment on the bath you made them have last night.

THE "YOU OK, HUN?"

The dog-human friendship goes back a long way; they've gotten to know us pretty well over the years and are very attuned to our emotions. Amazingly, your fuzzy friend can actually smell your feelings, especially ones like fear and distress. They don't like it when you're upset and so follow you around, giving you even more reassuring kisses than usual and resting their head on you to make sure you know they've got your back.

THE LIP LICK
v v v v v v v v v v v v

If you're frying a juicy steak, and your hound is watching you intensely and licking their lips, then it's not hard to guess what's going on in their mind. But what if there is no food around? Dogs often lick their lips when they are stressed or anxious, so check to see if you can figure out what's bothering them. If they lick their lips constantly, then it might be a sign they need to go to the doggy dentist.

THE HUMP

+ ✗ + ✗ + ✗ + ✗ +

Everyone knows that one dog who seems to enjoy embarrassing their human by joyfully humping everything in sight—other dogs, furniture, legs—despite the fact they've had the op. This behavior is actually quite common in dogs and is often about showing dominance or burning excess energy, rather than anything more, er, kinky. Though try telling that to the lady on the train whose large handbag has attracted your dog's enthusiastic attentions. Awkward!

THE FOOT WARMER

This slightly peculiar behavior is very specific—
some dogs love to perch on your pumps, while
others would never dream of it. If your dog
is a sneaker-sitter, it may be because you've
rewarded that behavior before, so they know
you like it. Alternatively, they might want to
be as close to you as possible to show how
much they love you or because something is
scaring them. So your dog might be thinking
either, "You're the best!" or, "FIREWORKS!!!"

THE HALF WAG

Don't be one of those basic humans who thinks waggy tail equals happy dog. As any hound will tell you, it's far more sophisticated than that. Doggy vision is very attuned to movement, so tail speak is a great way to get a point across. Two-legged companions will want to check out the rest of their friend's body language to get the message, but a short, slow, side-to-side wag halfway up can be a tell-tail sign that your dog is unsure or concerned about something.

THE WINDSHIELD WIPER

Wagging is very much a method of communication, and research has shown that dogs don't move their tails much when they are on their own—it would be like a human talking to the furniture. When your best friend's tail is going from side to side like a windshield wiper in a downpour, it's a clear sign to everyone around that this pooch is full of energy and ready to play! And perhaps, depending on the size of your furry buddy, an indication that you should hold on tight to any nearby family heirlooms.

THE "WHALE EYE"

Our doggy chums find this expression confusing, as they don't see what they have in common with large aquatic mammals. It's actually a phrase used by dog trainers to describe the way some breeds will keep their eyes big and round and turn their head to the side while still looking at something. This leaves a crescent of the white of their eye visible on the outer edge and usually means they feel scared or threatened.

THE BACKWARDS EARS

Dogs use their ears to say a lot. It obviously depends on the shape of your pooch's ears, but flattening them against their head and turning them backwards usually indicates fear. It also can mean defensive aggression. Generally, the further back from their normal position, the more worried the dog. Ears that are flattened but not against the head can mean your dog is sad or pining for something (maybe all the treats are gone!). And some dogs put their ears back and down when they are particularly enjoying a pet.

THE FORWARD EARS

This is a doggy who is really paying attention! Breeds with pointy ears are especially good at this, whereas a floppy-eared guy will slightly lift their ears too. If their paws are also pointing forward, it usually indicates a dog is interested in something and ready to play. If the dog is standing still and seems to be concentrating, that means they've heard something interesting far away—perhaps they are really looking forward to barking at the postman.

THE RADAR TAIL

A doggy wagging its tail around in an almost circular pattern can mean, "Scanning, scanning!" You may well notice it when your dog is hunting for their tennis ball or trying to figure out if their favorite toy is under the sofa. It looks a bit like radar searching the seabed and is a sign of intense concentration and unbridled joy.

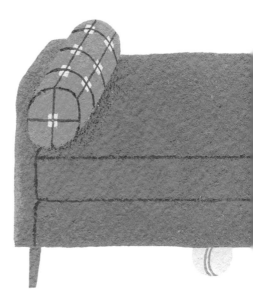

THE KARAOKE PERFORMANCE

Some dogs have a singsong bark when they are really excited about something. It's probably not going to get them a spot on *The X-Factor*, but it can be an indication that they are thrilled to see you and missed you so much when you were at work or out of the room for five minutes. Or they may be simply full of happy anticipation for the treat or walk they are pretty sure is about to come their way.

THE FAKE STEAL
+ ✗ + ✗ + ✗ + ✗ + + ✗ + ✗ +

This is often the go-to strategy of a bored doggo who's hoping you'll give them a game. The hopeful mutt will grab a sock or something they are pretty sure you're going to want back and stand there looking in your direction. When they're sure you've noticed, they take off, initiating a game of chase. If you don't like slobbery socks or giving your dog the satisfaction, you might want to teach them the "Drop it" command or distract them with a toy.

THE TAIL TUCK

The image of an unhappy or worried dog with its tail between its legs is such a recognizable one that we even use it as an expression to refer to people (to the slight confusion of our canines, who are always wondering how we manage without tails anyway). A scared or nervous pooch really will tuck their tail right underneath them, often while also licking their lips and looking to you for reassurance. Maybe they heard you say, "Vet," or are worried about what will happen when you find out what they've done to your new running shoes…

THE CARPET SCRATCHER

The urge to scratch and dig is still hardwired into our doggies' DNA from their wild days and pops up from time to time for a few different reasons. One theory is that they used to have a bit of a dig around at bedtime to make their sleeping area warmer or more comfortable, so if they are repeatedly pawing at their new dog bed, that might have something to do with it. On the other paw, because dogs have sweat glands on their feet, some think that it's a more indoor-friendly way to mark their territory.

THE COWER

A cowering dog is using the full menu of "This is not cool, guys" signs available to them. Their tail will probably be tucked under, their ears flattened, and their body down low, as they try to make themselves as small as possible. Even if your friend has gotten the wrong end of the throwing stick, and there's nothing to be scared of, you need to give them space and recognize that they are spooked right now. Be patient and kind as you try to work out what's bothering them.

THE TURNED BACK

Despite having been buddies for thousands of years, there are still some areas in which dog and human etiquette is still not quite in sync, and things can get lost in translation. Your furry friend doesn't realize that you might think their turned back is a sign of boredom or disdain, because they're actually saying, "I totally trust you not to be mean or eat my food, so I don't have to keep an eye on you." Or alternatively, "There's a spot I can't reach above my tail, kinda itchy; could you just . . . ?"

THE BIG SIGH

A well-timed sigh can say a lot, no matter what your species! There are a lot of reasons your pooch might exhale expressively. At the end of a long walk or playtime, or when lying down in their bed, it is likely to be a sign of contentment, though it can also signify frustration or

disappointment. If they are looking at you at the same time, perhaps they want to make a point about being ignored in favor of your phone or an unsatisfactory new brand of dog food. You could say that doggies can be passive-aggressive too!

THE STALK

Leaning forward, body low, nose pointing straight out, sniffing for prey…your doggy might be very fond of their home comforts but our pooches haven't forgotten all their wild habits! Of course, your dog knows their dinner will be delivered

in a bowl, and they aren't going to have to track it across the prairies, but sometimes they still like to pretend they are going on a good old-fashioned hunt. Even though, yes, it is a butterfly, and no, they won't be able to catch it.

THE FAITHFUL SHADOW

○○○○○○○○○○○○○○○○○○○ ○○○○○○○○○○○○○○○○○

Humans have bred dogs over thousands of years
to be our faithful companions, so it's no surprise
that they want to be with us. And, of course, we
love hanging out with them too. But what if your
little buddy literally won't let you out of their

sight? This is often a sign they are looking to you for help—maybe they are desperate to go out for a pee, there's a scary thunderstorm coming, or they feel unwell. If you've tried to help and explained that it's getting a little weird, and they still won't leave you alone, they may be suffering from separation anxiety, so check in with the vet.

THE SCENT ROLL

The average pooch has fifty times more olfactory receptors than you, and their brain is around forty times better at processing smells. Their nose is an incredibly sensitive instrument that gives them lots of information about the world around them. So *why* do some of our pets love to roll in the poo of other animals?! If it

smells gross to us, surely it's horrendous for them? This is a mystery that may never be solved. Plenty of predators, like wolves, lions, and coyotes, are known to do this in the wild too, but experts don't have a definitive explanation.

THE BURIED TREASURE

Some dogs think that storing things underground is a great idea. It's not hard to guess that this technique was used by wild dogs to hide food so they could come back to it later. But why then does your dog bury their chew toy or your socks? Pooches who live with other pooches may be more likely to do this—it's their way of saying, "That's mine!" It can occasionally be a stress response, the doggy equivalent of hoarding, so you might want to check that nothing is bothering them. Or they might have just decided that toys look better with added soil.

German
Shepherd *p.7*

Bichon Frise
p.9

Greyhound
p.10

Italian Greyhound
p.12

Labradoodle
p.14

American Pit
Bull Terrier *p.17*

Beagle
p.18

Dalmatian
p.20

Vizsla
p.23

Airedale
Terrier *p.24*

Bull Terrier
p.27

Miniature Poodle
and Miniature
Pinscher *p.29*

Chinese Crested
Dog *p.31*

Dachshund
p.32

Miniature
Schnauzer *p.34*

Basenji
p.37

Basset
Hound *p.39*

Welsh Corgi
p.41

Jack Russell
Terrier *p.43*

Bluetick
Coonhound *p.44*

Chihuahua
p.46

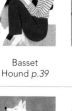

Saluki
p.49

West Siberian
Laika *p.50*

Labrador
Retriever *p.53*

Dachshund
and Great
Dane *p.54*

Australian
Shepherd *p.56*

Chow Chow
p.58

Shiba Inu
p.61

Weimaraner
p.62

English
Bulldog *p.65*

Jack Russell
Terrier p.67

Italian
Greyhound and
Borzoi p.68

Schipperke
p.71

Boston
Terrier p.72

Shih Tzu
p.75

Poodle
p.76

Siberian
Husky p.79

Labrador
Retriever p.81

Komondor
p.82

Australian Cattle
Dog p.85

Ibizan Hound
p.86

Pug
p.88

Pekingese
p.91

Old English
Sheepdog p.92

Cavalier
King Charles
Spaniel p.94

Affenpinscher
p.97

Xoloitzcuintle
(Mexican Hairless
Dog) p.98

Pharaoh
Hound p.101

Scottish
Deerhound
p.103

Norwich
Terrier p.104

Brussels
Griffon p.107

Bull Terrier
p.108

Cirneco
dell'Etna p.111

Chihuahua
p.113

Poodle
p.115

Afghan
Hound p.116

German
Shorthaired
Pointer p.118

Bedlington
Terrier p.120

Irish Setter
p.123

West Highland
White Terrier p.124

ABOUT THE AUTHOR

Liz Marvin is a writer and editor based by the sea on England's south coast. She has previously written *How to Be More Tree*, *The Secret Lives of Animals*, and *The Windowsill Gardener*. She enjoys long walks, jumping in water, and sleeping in the daytime, and would make an excellent Labrador.

ABOUT THE ILLUSTRATOR

Yelena Bryksenkova is an illustrator and fine artist working primarily by hand using Acryla gouache and colored pencils on paper. She studied illustration at the Maryland Institute College of Art in Baltimore, Maryland, and the Academy of Arts, Architecture, and Design in Prague, Czech Republic. Yelena's work often features welcoming interior and exterior spaces, with scenes of daily life, nature, and people and animals in repose. She lives and works in Montreal, Canada.